Japanese Recipes

An Easy Guide to Japanese Sweet Mochi

BY

Daniel Humphreys

License Notes

No part of this Book can be reproduced in any form or by any means including print, electronic, scanning or photocopying unless prior permission is granted by the author.

All ideas, suggestions and guidelines mentioned here are written for informative purposes. While the author has taken every possible step to ensure accuracy, all readers are advised to follow information at their own risk. The author cannot be held responsible for personal and/or commercial damages in case of misinterpreting and misunderstanding any part of this Book

Table of Contents

Introduction

A mochi is a Japanese dessert which is made of very glutinous rice. The rice is made into a paste form and then shaped in the desired way. Mochi in Japan is made in a traditional ceremony which is known as mochitsuki. This mochi is not only eaten at New Year's Eve or during the New Year times but it is so common it is eaten all year long.

The traditional method of preparing the mochi was done by soaking the rice overnight and then steaming it. The steamed rice was then mashed by a traditional equipment that the Japanese had. They had to continuously mash and stir the mixture with 2 people alternatively performing this task very carefully. The mashed rice was then served and eaten immediately.

The modern preparation of mochi is comparatively easy and simple as no special equipment is required to finish this job. It can be easily done with utensils you have at home. The modern method involves preparing the mochi from the flour of sweet rice. The flour is mixed with the water and baking powder and then kept in the microwave for as long as it takes to set. It might take up to 2 minutes or sometimes may take more time. The sticky dough is removed from the microwave oven and allowed to set.

The next step depends upon the person making the mochi; you may want to roll out this mochi from the microwave oven and dust with potato starch to eat plain and simple or you may wish to make it fancier and tastier by making a nice filling to go with it.

There are various kinds of fillings that can be made to go along with this Japanese mochi. For instance, it can be filled with either a cream cheese filling, or a dark chocolate filling, Nutella chocolate filling, raspberry jam filling, strawberry jam filling, chocolate chip filling, butter filling, whole strawberry filling, a nice filling of cheese or it can be served plain as well. Traditionally, mochi was served just by itself which is the most basic preparation.

Chapter 01: Easy Butter Mochi

Recipe 01: Easy Mochi

This easy mochi is a lovely Japanese snack for New Year's Eve and it is a wonderful, sweet and chewy dessert.

Preparation time: 3 hours 35 minutes.

Makes: 8 servings.

Ingredients:

- Sweetened red bean paste- 1 cup
- Sweet rice flour, mochiko- 1 cup
- Green tea powder, matcha- 1 teaspoon
- Water- 1 cup
- White sugar- ¼ cup
- Cornstarch for rolling the dough- ½ cup

Directions:

Wrap the sweetened red bean paste and freeze it for 3 hours.

Mix the sweet rice flour and the green tea powder in a bowl.

Add the water and the white sugar.

Mix the ingredients until smooth.

Cover with plastic wrap.

Cook this mixture in the microwave oven for at least 3 minutes.

Remove red bean paste from the freezer and divide into 8 equal balls.

Dust surface with cornstarch and while the mochi is hot from the oven, start making balls the size of one tablespoons.

Flatten the mochi and add in the red bean paste in the center; then, enclose the mochi so as to completely cover the paste.

Sprinkle the mochi with some more cornstarch to prevent sticking.

Recipe 02: Microwave Mochi

This mochi can be easily made in the microwave. It is sweet and tempting.

Preparation time: 15 minutes

Makes: 25 servings

Ingredients:

- Mochiko- 1 ½ cups
- White sugar- 1 cup
- Water- 1 ½ cups
- Distilled white vinegar- 2 drops
- Potato starch- ½ cup
- White sugar- ¼ cup
- Salt- ¼ teaspoon

Directions:

Take a bowl and mix in the mochiko, white sugar and the water until they are mixed well.

Now add the vinegar drops to soften the mixture.

Put the bowl in the microwave for about 8 to 10 minutes on high heat.

Remove and let it cool.

In another bowl add in the potato starch, sugar and salt and mix.

Cut the mochi into pieces with the knife and roll them in the potato starch mixture.

Recipe 03: Ono Butter Mochi

This is a Hawaiian recipe for mochi and is made with butter and coconut with a base of rice. This dessert is great for all kinds of tropical parties.

Preparation time: 1 hour 15 minutes

Makes: 12 servings

Ingredients:

- Mochiko- 1 pound
- White sugar- 2 ½ cups
- Baking powder- 1 teaspoons
- Melted butter- ½ cup
- Milk- 3 cups
- Eggs- 5
- Vanilla extract- 1 teaspoon
- Sweetened flaked coconut- 1 cup

Directions:

Preheat your oven to 350 degrees F.

Take a bowl and add in the eggs, milk and the vanilla extract; whisk together.

In another bowl combine the dry Ingredients: rice flour, sugar and the baking powder.

Mix the dry and the wet ingredients until well combined.

Now mix in the melted butter and the flaked coconut.

Pour into prepared baking dish and put in the oven to bake.

Bake for an hour, cut into squares and serve.

Recipe 04: Chi Chi Dango Mochi

This recipe of chi chi dango mochi is a traditional Japanese dessert. It is soft and chewy and great for picnics and parties.

Preparation time: 1 hour 36 minutes

Makes: 36 servings

Ingredients:

- Mochiko- 1 pound
- White sugar- 2 ½ cups
- Baking powder- 1 teaspoon
- Water- 2 cups
- Vanilla extract- 1 teaspoon
- Coconut milk- 1 can
- Red food color- ¼ teaspoon
- Potato starch- 1 ½ cups

Directions:

Preheat your oven to 350 degrees F.

Mix together the rice flour, sugar and the baking powder.

In another bowl add in the water, coconut milk, vanilla and the red food coloring.

Combine the flour mixture and the coconut milk mixture.

Mix the ingredients and pour them into a baking dish.

Bake for 1 hour and allow to cool.

Dust surface with potato starch and place the pan on the potato starch.

Cut into pieces and serve.

Recipe 05: Butter Mochi Cake

This butter mochi cake has a rich and buttery taste. Butter mochi is a western version of the traditional Japanese mochi dessert.

Preparation time: 1 hour 40 minutes

Serves: 12

Ingredients:

- Melted unsalted butter- ½ cup
- White sugar- 1 ¼ cup
- Eggs- 3
- Vanilla extract- 1 teaspoon
- Rice flour- 3 cups
- Baking powder- 1 teaspoon
- Milk- 3 cups
- Red bean paste- 1 can

Directions:

Preheat oven to 350 F.

In a bowl mix in the butter, sugar, eggs, vanilla extract and the milk.

Now add in the rice flour and the baking powder.

Combine and then pour the mixture into a baking dish.

Drop little spoonfuls of the red bean paste on top of the batter.

Bake for 1 hour and 10 minutes or until the cake springs back when pressed.

Cool and serve.

Chapter 02: Chocolate Mochi Recipes

Recipe 06: Dark Chocolate Truffle Mochi

These dark chocolate truffle mochi are soft and chewy glutinous rice dough filled with the amazing dark chocolates.

Preparation time: 30 minutes

Makes: 16 mochis

Ingredients:

- Dark chocolate- 250 grams
- Unsalted butter- 2 tablespoons
- Heavy cream- ½ cup
- Rum- 2 tablespoons
- Vanilla extract- 1 teaspoon
- Cocoa powder- ½ cup
- 1 ½ cups potato starch
- Water- 2/3 cup
- Sugar- ¼ cup
- Rice flour- 1 cup

Directions:

First make the ganache.

Chop the chocolate and the butter in a bowl.

In a sauce pan add the cream and bring it to a boil.

Pour this cream in the chocolate and butter; stir until combined.

Now add in the rum and the vanilla extract and stir until smooth.

Cool and then form balls and coat them in the cocoa powder.

Dust surface with the potato starch

Mix the rice flour and the sugar in a bowl and add in the water. Mix.

Microwave it for 2 minutes.

Let it set, and then roll out the dough and place the ganache balls in the center and enclose the dough so to cover the ganache.

Serve!

Recipe 07: Chocolate Mochi

This a traditional Hawaiian Japanese recipe of a Japanese cake made with chocolate.

Preparation time: 15 minutes

Serves: 10

Ingredients:

- Mochiko- 2 cups
- White sugar- 2 cups
- Baking soda- 1 tablespoons
- Semi-sweet chocolate chips- 1 cup
- Evaporated milk- 2 cans
- Melted margarine- ½ cup
- Vanilla extract- 2 teaspoons
- Eggs- 2

Directions:

In a large bowl mix the mochiko, sugar and the baking soda.

Melt the margarine and the chocolate chips and then add in the milk, vanilla extract and the eggs. Mix until smooth.

Mix well and pour into a baking dish and put to bake in preheated oven at 350 F for about 45 minutes. Serve!

Recipe 08: Chocolate Mochi Snack Cake

This Japanese recipe of a chocolate mochi snack cake is full of chocolate and has a soft and chewy texture. It is perfect for an afternoon snack.

Preparation time: 20 minutes

Serves: 7

Ingredients:

- Rice flour- 2 cups
- White sugar- 2 cups
- Baking soda- 1 tablespoon
- Unsalted butter- ½ cup
- Chocolate chips- 1 cup
- Vanilla extract- 2 teaspoons
- Evaporated milk- 24 ounces
- Eggs- 2

Directions:

Preheat oven to 350 F.

In a bowl mix the rice flour, baking soda and the sugar and set aside.

In a sauce pan add the butter and chocolate chips and melt them both.

With a beater now beat in the evaporated milk, vanilla extract and the eggs in the chocolate mixture and mix the ingredients.

Now add in the dry Ingredients: the flour, baking soda and the sugar; mix until incorporated.

Pour batter in a dish and bake for 40 minutes.

Recipe 09: Chocolate Mochi Mug Cake

This chocolate mochi mug cake is perfect for late night cravings. It is extremely simple and quick to make.

Preparation time: 5 minutes

Makes: 1 mug cake

Ingredients:

- Sweet rice flour- 2 tablespoons
- Sugar- 1 tablespoon
- Cocoa powder- ½ tablespoon
- Baking powder- 1/8 teaspoon
- Vegetable oil- ½ tablespoon
- Nonfat milk- 2 tablespoons

Directions:

In a mug add the sweet rice flour, sugar, cocoa powder and the baking powder.

Now mix in the wet ingredients until batter is smooth.

Put in the microwave for 60 seconds.

Serve immediately

Recipe 10: Yummy Chocolate Mochi Cake

This chocolate mochi cake is full of chocolate flavor and has a rich and gooey taste.

Preparation time: 15 minutes

Serves: 16

Ingredients:

- Mochiko- 1 cup
- Sugar- 1 cup
- Baking soda- 1 ½ teaspoon
- Butter- ¼ cup
- Chocolate- ½ cup
- Evaporated milk- 1 can
- Vanilla extract- 1 teaspoon
- Egg- 1

Directions:

Preheat your oven to 350 degrees F.

Mix in the mochiko, sugar and the baking soda.

In a sauce pan melt the chocolate and the butter.

Using a beater beat in the evaporated milk, vanilla extract and the egg and mix.

Now add the dry Ingredients: the mochiko, sugar and the baking soda and mix well.

Pour the batter into a baking dish; bake for 50-60 minutes.

Cool and serve!

Recipe 11: Chocolate Butter Mochi

This chocolate butter mochi has a delightful chocolate flavor and is very easy to make.

Preparation time: 10 minutes

Serves: 7

Ingredients:

- Mochiko- 16 ounce
- Sugar- 2 cups
- Baking soda- 1 teaspoon
- Cocoa powder- 3 tablespoons
- Butter- ½ cup
- Chocolate chips- 1 ½ cups
- Evaporated milk- 1 can
- Coconut milk- 1 can
- Eggs-2
- Vanilla extract- 2 teaspoons

Directions:

Pre-heat your oven to 350 degrees F.

Mix the mochiko, sugar and baking soda in a bowl; set aside.

Melt the butter and chocolate chips in a saucepan on low heat.

Beat in the evaporated milk, coconut milk, eggs and the vanilla extract until well combined.

Add in the dry ingredients and mix until well combined.

Pour the mixture into a prepared baking dish and bake for 40 minutes.

Chapter 03: Strawberry Mochi Cakes

Recipe 12: Strawberry Cream Cheese Mochi

Strawberry cream cheese mochi is a very wonderful recipe for evening parties. The cream cheese filling along with the rice flour gives it a nice kick.

Preparation time: 30 minutes

Makes: 2 dozen

Ingredients:

- Powdered sugar- 2 tablespoon
- Cream cheese- 4 ounce
- Almond extract- ½ teaspoon
- Water- 2 ¾ cup
- Sugar- 1 cup
- Mochiko- 16 ounce
- Almond extract- 1 teaspoon
- Katakuirko- 1 teaspoon
- Strawberries- ½ cup

Directions:

Mix the powdered sugar, cream cheese and the almond extract until blended. Refrigerate.

In a sauce pan boil the water and add in the sugar to dissolve.

Start adding ¼ cup of mochiko at a time to the water mixture.

Now add the almond extract.

Dust the surface with karauirko and turn the mochiko onto it.

Roll the mochiko until flat. Divide.

Add the cream cheese filling on each mochiko and enclose it to cover completely.

Garnish with strawberries

Recipe 13: Strawberry Mochi

This strawberry mochi is made with strawberry juice so it has a very good flavor. It is a refreshing dessert.

Preparation time: 5 minutes

Makes: 2

Ingredients:

- Rice flour-1 cup
- Cane sugar- ¼ cup
- Water- 2/3 cup
- Cornstarch- ½ cup
- Strawberry juice- 3 tablespoons
- Strawberry jam- 12 tablespoons

Directions:

First, mix the rice flour, sugar, strawberry juice and water. Mix them to form a thick paste.

Then cook it in the microwave for 2 minutes.

Cook more if required.

When done, cool the dough and flatten it.

Dust surface with cornstarch and make 12 mochis from the dough.

Put at least one tablespoon of strawberry jam on each mochi and enclose it.

Serve!

Recipe 14: Strawberry Daifuku Mochi Recipe

This is a delightful Japanese mochi recipe filled with delicious bits of sweet strawberries!

Preparation time: 30 minutes

Serves: 10

Ingredients:

- Strawberries- 10
- Anko- 100 to 120 grams
- Shiratamako (rice flour)- 100 grams
- Sugar- 50 grams
- Cold water- 150 ml
- Katarukiko (potato starch)- plenty for dusting the surface

Directions:

Rinse and dry the strawberries.

Coat the strawberries with the anko paste and cover them

Refrigerate.

In a bowl, add the rice flour, water and sugar; stir to dissolve.

Put it in the microwave for 2 minutes or more until it is cooked.

Dust surface with plenty of potato starch and pour the rice flour mixture on top of it so that it does not stick.

Roll the dough and using a pastry cutter cut the dough into 10 equal pieces.

Remove the coated strawberries from the fridge and put one strawberry in each piece of the dough and enclose properly to cover the strawberry inside.

Let them set and serve!

Recipe 15: Strawberry Mochi with Red Bean

The addition of red bean to this strawberry mochi gives it a unique flavor.

Preparation time: 25 minutes

Makes: 6 large mochi bites

Ingredients:

- Red bean paste-½ cup plus one tablespoon
- Strawberries- 6 large
- Rice flour- ¾ cup
- Water- 100 ml
- Sugar- 2 tablespoons
- Potato starch or cornstarch- to roll

Directions:

Divide the red bean paste into 6 portions.

Coat each strawberry in the red bean paste.

Dust surface of cutting board with potato starch or cornstarch.

For the mochiko, mix the rice flour, water and the sugar and stir until dissolved.

Microwave this mixture for 2 minutes or more until it is set.

Pour out this sticky mochiko mixture onto the surface dusted with potato starch or cornstarch.

Roll out the mochiko and divide it into 6 equal portions.

Place the coated red bean strawberries from the fridge; place on each mochiko and enclose.

Serve it cold!

Recipe 16: Chilled Strawberry Soup with Chocolaty Strawberry Rice Balls

This recipe looks appealing just by the name of it. The chilled soup along with the chocolate balls coated with strawberry tastes divine.

Preparation time: 30 minutes

Serves: 2

Ingredients:

- Sugar- 3 tablespoons
- Water- 3 tablespoons
- Strawberry puree- 1 cup
- Plain yoghurt- 1/3 cup
- Seltzer water- 3 tablespoons
- Lemon juice- 1
- Rice flour- ½ cup
- Powdered sugar- 3 tablespoons
- Strawberry puree- 5 tablespoons
- Chocolate chips-20

Directions:

Take a saucepan and add the sugar and water; heat until the sugar is completely dissolved.

Now take a blender and add in the strawberry puree, plain yoghurt, seltzer water and lemon juice; blend.

Add the melted sugar and blend again.

Put in the fridge to chill.

For the chocolate sweet rice balls, boil water in a pan.

Mix the rice flour and the powdered sugar, and add in the strawberry puree until it forms a sticky dough. Knead until dough is no longer sticky.

Roll balls from the dough and press chocolate chips in each ball.

When the water is boiled add the balls in the boiling water and cook until the balls float on top of the water.

Add these balls in the chilled soup from the fridge and serve cold!

Chapter 04: Japanese Mochi Flavor Variety

Recipe 17: Warabi Mochi Recipe

This recipe contains two of Japan's most common ingredients; they are known as warabi mochiko and kinako.

Preparation time: 30 minutes

Makes: 24

Ingredients:

- Warabi mochiko- 60 grams
- Lukewarm water- 1 cup
- Sugar- 50 grams
- Kinako- 30 grams

Directions:

In a bowl, slowly add the water to the warabi mochiko; mix until smooth. Then, add the sugar until well combined.

Take a baking sheet and sprinkle the kinako onto the baking sheet.

Heat the warabi mochiko mixture in a saucepan and stir until it becomes thick.

Pour the warabi mochiko mixture on top of the sprinkled kinaku and let it set.

Pour more kinaku on top.

Using a sharp knife cut into squares after it has completely cooled and set

Serve!

Recipe 18: Pumpkin Mochi

The addition of pumpkin makes these Japanese sweet mochis a bit different.

Preparation time: 1 hour 10 minutes

Makes: 12 servings

Ingredients:

- Mochiko- 2 ½ cups
- Baking powder- 2 teaspoons
- White sugar-2 cups
- Eggs- 4
- Pumpkin puree- 1 can
- Condensed milk- 1 can
- Melted butter- 1 cup
- Vanilla extract- 2 teaspoons

Directions:

Preheat your oven to 350 F.

In a large bowl mix in the mochiko, sugar and the baking powder. Set aside.

In another bowl mix in the eggs, pumpkin puree, condensed milk, melted butter and the vanilla extract.

Mix together all ingredients and pour into the mochiko mixture; combine.

Pour the batter into a baking dish and bake for 50-60 minutes.

Allow to cool before serving.

Recipe 19: Guamanian Mochi

This guamanian mochi is mostly eaten in the lands of hawaii. It is soft, chewy and sticky and tastes delicious.

Preparation time: 40 minutes

Makes: 48 servings

Ingredients:

- Mochiko- 2 cups
- White sugar- 1 ¾ cups
- Baking soda- 1 tablespoon
- Eggs- 2
- Evaporated milk- 1 can
- Coconut milk- 1 can
- Vanilla extract-1 teaspoon
- Melted butter- ¼ cup

Directions:

Preheat your oven to 350 F.

In a bowl mix the mochiko, white sugar and the baking soda.

In another bowl beat in the eggs, evaporated milk, coconut milk, vanilla extract and the melted butter. Mix properly.

Now mix the mochiko mixture and the eggs mixture properly so that all the ingredients are incorporated together.

Pour the batter into a baking dish and bake for 25-30 minutes.

Cool and then serve!

Recipe 20: Broiled Mochi with Nori Seaweed

This recipe is very unique because it makes use of more novel ingredients like the Nori, and the mochi is also broiled in this special preparation.

Preparation time: 17 minutes

Makes: 8 servings

Ingredients:

- Frozen mochi squares- 8
- Soy sauce- ½ cup
- Nori- 1 sheet

Directions:

Preheat your oven to 450 F.

Cut the mochis into square shapes and dip into the soy sauce.

Place these dipped mochi squares on the baking sheet and bake for about 5 minutes.

Cut the nori seaweed into thin strips.

Over medium heat, put the seaweed strips in a saucepan and warm for 1-2 minutes. Cool them.

Wrap each mochi with these thin seaweed strips and then serve!

Recipe 21: Chocolate Glazed Mochi Doughnuts

This Japanese inspired sweet dish is made with rice cakes along with the richness of chocolate.

Preparation time: 30 minutes

Makes: 10 servings

Ingredients:

- Mochiko- 2 cups
- Milk- 3 tablespoons
- Milk- ½ cup
- Egg- 1
- Sugar- ¼ cup
- Melted butter- 9 tablespoons
- Baking powder- 1 ½ tablespoons
- Vanilla extract- 1 teaspoon
- Warm water to knead- as needed
- Coconut milk- 1/3 cup
- Dark chocolate- 12 ounces
- Powdered sugar- 2 cups

Directions:

Mix ¼ of the mochiko and the milk. Microwave until they are set.

In another bowl add the rest of the mochiko, milk, egg, sugar, baking powder and the vanilla extract. Mix well.

Add the cooled microwave mochiko to the uncooked mochiko.

Knead the entire dough well.

Roll out the dough while dusting with flour and cut into doughnut shapes.

In a pot heat the oil and fry the doughnuts until golden.

For the chocolate sauce, melt the dark chocolate and add in the coconut milk. Stir.

Cool and drizzle over the doughnuts.

Sprinkle with powdered sugar.

Recipe 22: Dark Chocolate Mochi Truffles

These one bite mochi truffles are almost everyones favorite and greatly enjoyed by kids.

Preparation time: 30 minutes

Makes: 16

Ingredients:

- Dark chocolate- 250 grams
- Cocoa powder- ½ cup
- Unsalted butter- 2 tablespoons
- Heavy cream- ½ cup
- Vanilla extract- 1 teaspoon
- Corn flour- 1 ½ cups
- Rice flour- 2 cups
- Sugar- ¼ cup
- Water- 2/3 cup

Directions:

To make the ganache, start by melting the dark chocolate and the butter together in a double boiler.

Stir in the cream and then add the vanilla extract.

Let cool.

Shape the ganache into balls and coat them with cocoa powder.

Dust your surface with the corn starch.

To make the mochi mix the rice flour, sugar and water and keep in the microwave until they are set.

Roll out the mochi and divide into portions.

Enclose in the ganache balls and cover.

Serve!

Recipe 23: Microwave Mochi With Chocolate Chips

This recipe is extremely easy and very simple with only a few ingredients.

Preparation time: 15 minutes

Makes: 25 servings

Ingredients:

- Mochiko- 1 ½ cups
- White sugar- 1 cup
- Water- 1 ½ cups
- Vinegar- 2 drops
- Chocolate chips- 25
- Potato starch- for dusting
- Sugar- ¼ cup
- Salt- ¼ teaspoon

Directions:

For the rice cake, mix the mochiko, white sugar, vinegar and the water.

Microwave it until it is set.

Now roll this mochi onto the potato starch, sugar and the salt until coated properly.

Cut in pieces and shape into balls while putting in each ball a chocolate chip.

Serve!

Recipe 24: Chocolate Mochi Bars

These chocolate mochi bars are the perfect afternoon snack. You can even have them in your breakfast with tea.

Preparation time: 15 minutes

Makes: 20

Ingredients:

- Mochiko- 2 cups
- White sugar- 1 cup
- Baking soda- ½ teaspoon
- Egg- 1
- Evaporated milk- 1 can
- Chocolate chips- ½ cup
- Vanilla extract- 1 teaspoon
- Butter- ½ stick

Directions:

Preheat your oven to 350 F.

Mix the mochiko, sugar and the baking powder.

In another bowl mix the egg, evaporated milk and the vanilla extract.

Melt together the butter and the chocolate chips and add to the egg mixture. Mix well.

Now mix in the mochiko mixture to the wet ingredients.

Pour batter into a dish and bake for 25-30 minutes.

Recipe 25: Simple Mochi Recipe

This recipe is one of the oldest recipes of the Japanese sweet dish.

Preparation time: 2 minutes

Makes: 10

Ingredients:

- Mochiko- 1 cup
- Water- 1 cup
- Sugar- ¼ cup
- Vanilla ice cream
- Potato starch- for dusting

Directions:

In a bowl mix the mochiko, water and the sugar.

Microwave them for 2 to 4 minutes until the mochi is completely set.

Dust the surface with potato starch.

Roll out the mochi and divide into portions.

Scoop out ice cream into each part and enclose.

Serve immediately

Recipe 26: Sweet Mochi Recipe

In this recipe, the green tea ice cream is used which adds to the flavor of these mochis.

Preparation time: 10 minutes

Serves 5

Ingredients:

- Mochiko- 1 cup
- Water- ¾ cup
- Sugar- 2 cups
- Corn starch- for dusting
- Green tea ice cream- 5 scoops

Directions:

In a bowl add the mochiko, water and the sugar and put in the microwave for about 2 to 4 minutes or until the mochi is completely set.

Dust the surface with cornstarch and roll out the mochi.

Divide into equal portions and scoop out the green tea ice cream and enclose.

Serve cold.

Conclusion

The aim of this book was to introduce to you the best and easiest way to prepare Japanese mochi. It is easy to follow and master the art of these Japanese sweet mochis but some valid points and tips should be noted.

The quantity of all the ingredients should be noted with great care. The most important ingredient of this Japanese sweet dish is the rice flour. If the consistency of the rice flour is okay, then your whole sweet dish will be perfect but if the consistency of the rice flour is not accurate it can ruin your whole desert.

The rice flour should not be very dry or otherwise it will be very hard to eat. It should not be very sticky otherwise it will stick to the hands. If the rice flour is not made properly then no filling inside it would stay.

It can get quite messy to eat if the filling inside starts to fall on your clothes and hands. This can happen if the rice flour is not made correctly.

The people of Japan are very polite and they put a lot of emphasis on sharing their food and drink, giving everyone a share of their own food. They follow proper rules while and before eating and prefer to eat meals with patience and start their meals with their chopsticks. Usually the food is served with a stainless-steel spoon in the center of the dish.

Thus, all these things should be kept in mind when making the Japanese food. All the pros and cons have been mentioned. It is easy but all the rules should be properly followed and the ingredients must not be substituted with other ingredients. You should only begin if you have skill, time and all the ingredients available!

Author's Afterthoughts

Thanks ever so much to each of my cherished readers for investing the time to read this book!

I know you could have picked from many other books but you chose this one. So a big thanks for downloading this book and reading all the way to the end.

If you enjoyed this book or received value from it, I'd like to ask you for a favor. Please take a few minutes to post an honest and heartfelt review on Amazon.com. Your support does make a difference and helps to benefit other people.

Thanks!

Daniel Humphreys

About the Author

Daniel Humphreys

Many people will ask me if I am German or Norman, and my answer is that I am 100% unique! Joking aside, I owe my cooking influence mainly to my mother who was British! I can certainly make a mean Sheppard's pie, but when it comes to preparing Bratwurst sausages and drinking beer with friends, I am also all in!

I am taking you on this culinary journey with me and hope you can appreciate my diversified background. In my 15 years career as a chef, I never had a dish returned to me by one of clients, so that should say something about me! Actually, I will take that back. My worst critic is my four years old son, who refuses to taste anything that is green color. That shall pass, I am sure.

My hope is to help my children discover the joy of cooking and sharing their creations with their loved ones, like I did all my life. When you develop a passion for cooking and my suspicious is that you have one as well, it usually sticks for life. The best advice I can give anyone as a professional chef is invest. Invest your time, your heart in each meal you are creating. Invest also a little money in good cooking hardware and quality ingredients. But most of all enjoy every meal you prepare with YOUR friends and family!

Printed in Great Britain
by Amazon